Show Me
DOGS

My First Picture Encyclopedia

by Megan Cooley Peterson

Consultant:
Jennifer Zablotny, DVM
American Veterinary Medical Association

CAPSTONE PRESS
a capstone imprint

A+ Books are published by Capstone Press,
1710 Roe Crest Drive, North Mankato, Minnesota 56003.
www.capstonepub.com

Library of Congress Cataloging-in-Publication Data
Peterson, Megan Cooley.
  Show me dogs : my first picture encyclopedia / by Megan Cooley Peterson.
    p. cm. — (A+. my first picture encyclopedias)
  Summary: "Defines through text and photos core terms related to dogs"—Provided
    by publisher.
  ISBN 978-1-4296-8572-6 (library binding)
  ISBN 978-1-62065-195-7 (ebook PDF)
  1. Dogs–Encyclopedias. 2. Dog breeds–Encyclopedias. I. Title.
  SF422.P48 2013
  636.703—dc23   2012002681

Editorial Credits

Kristen Mohn, editor; Tracy Davies McCabe, designer; Svetlana Zhurkin, media researcher; Laura Manthe, production specialist

Photo Credits

123RF: Kelly Richardson, 11 (bottom left); Canine Good Citizen® photo © 2012 The American Kennel Club, Inc. Used with permission. Canine Good Citizen is a registered trademark of The American Kennel Club, Inc., 27 (middle); Capstone Studio: Karon Dubke, 11 (middle right); Dreamstime: Anna Utekhina, 29 (top), Cynoclub, 10 (top), Eriklam, back cover, 4 (bottom), Gabriel Blaj, 17 (middle), Grecu Mihail Alin, 29 (middle right), Jennifer Walz, 11 (top right), Jstaley401, 11 (bottom right), Lukas Blazek, 12 (bottom right), Manon Ringuette, 25 (middle), Oleksandr Bilozerov, 19 (middle), 29 (bottom right), Pixago, 16 (top), Tomáš Prokop, 13 (middle); iStockphoto: jclegg, 28 (top right), Jill Fromer, cover (bottom middle left), 25 (top right), Jodi Jacobson, 13 (top), Joe Michl, 27 (bottom right), John Kirk, 5 (bottom right), Jonathan Brizendine, 11 (top left), Micah Young, 24 (bottom right), Paolo Florendo, 20 (top right), PK-Photos, 22 (bottom right), Roberto A. Sanchez, 23 (middle left); Newscom: Digital Press Photos, 31 (bottom left); photo by Diane Lewis © 2003 The American Kennel Club, Inc. Used with permission., 26 (bottom right); PhotoAlto, 23 (top); Photodisc, 6 (bottom); Shutterstock: Alexey Stiop, 24 (top), Alistair Scott, 22 (top), Andrey Shtanko, 29 (middle left), Anna Hoychuk, cover (bottom left), aspen rock, 19 (top), Boris Djuranovic, 30 (top), clearviewstock, 31 (top), Colour, cover (bottom middle right), daseaford, 19 (bottom right), Denis Pepin, 5 (bottom middle), Dewayne Flowers, 18 (top left), dwphotos, 21 (top left), Elnur, cover (top), 1 (top), 28 (middle), Eric Isselée, 5 (top left and bottom left), 7 (top left and right, middle right, bottom middle and right), 8 (top left and middle, and bottom all), 9 (top left and right, bottom left and middle), 21 (bottom right), 29 (bottom left), Erik Lam, 6 (top left), 8 (top right), 10 (middle left), 11 (middle left), 15, foto Arts, 12 (left), FreeSoulProduction (dog paw prints), cover and throughout, Geoffrey Kuchera, 27 (bottom left), Golden Pixels, 20 (top left), Hannamariah, 12 (top right), IKO, 23 (bottom right), iofoto, 30 (middle right), IrinaK, 28 (bottom), James Clarke, 27 (top), Jason X. Pacheco, 21 (bottom left), Jeffrey Moore, 26 (bottom left), Jim Parkin, 30 (bottom), JStaley401, 10 (bottom), Julien, 17 (bottom left), Kelly Nelson, 31 (middle left), Kelly Richardson, 17 (top left), Kirk Geisler, 31 (middle right), Liliya Kulianionak, 5 (top right), Lobke Peers, 25 (top left), maminez, 16 (bottom right), Marcel Jancovic, 31 (bottom right), Margo Harrison, 6 (top right), Mark Herreid, 24 (bottom left), Matt Apps, 22 (bottom left), Maxim Kulko, 5 (middle left), Michael Pettigrew, 21 (top right), mitzy, 18 (bottom), Nancy Hixson, 16 (bottom left), Nikolai Pozdeev, cover (bottom right), Nikolai Tsvetkov, 7 (bottom left), 30 (bottom left), Phase4Photography, 18 (top right), Richard Semik, 4 (top), 13 (bottom), Sergey Lavrentev, 19 (bottom left), Sue McDonald, 23 (middle right), 25 (bottom), Susan Schmitz, cover (top front), 1 (top front), 9 (top middle and bottom right), 20 (bottom), 21 (middle left), Tom Biegalski, 10 (middle right), Ultrashock, 5 (middle right), V. J. Matthew, 21 (middle right), Viorel Sima, 7 (middle left), 14, Vlad Ageshin, 13 (back), vseb, 28 (top left), Willee Cole, 17 (top right), 26 (top), woodygraphs, 23 (bottom left), Zoltan Pataki, 17 (bottom right)

Note to Parents, Teachers, and Librarians

My First Picture Encyclopedias provide an early introduction to reference materials for young children. These accessible, visual encyclopedias support literacy development by building subject-specific vocabularies and research skills. Stimulating format, inviting content, and phonetic aids assist and encourage young readers.

Printed in the United States of America in North Mankato, Minnesota.

042012   006682CGF12

Table of Contents

What Are Dogs?

With their wagging tails and slobbery kisses, dogs are often called man's best friend. But what are dogs? Where did they come from?

mammal

(MAM-uhl)—a warm-blooded animal that has a backbone and feeds milk to its young; mammals also have hair and give live birth to their young

species

a group of animals with similar features; all dogs belong to the same species, called *Canis lupus familiaris*

evolve

(ih-VAHLV)—to change gradually; many of today's dogs evolved from the gray wolf

4

breed

a certain kind of dog; there are more than 400 different dog breeds

Labrador retriever

purebred

(PYOOR-bred)—having ancestors of the same breed

The Dog Family

wolf—a wild mammal that is related to the dog and hunts in groups for food

wolf

fox—a wild animal related to the dog, which has thick fur, a pointed nose and ears, and a bushy tail

fox

jackal (JAK-uhl)—a long-legged wild dog found in Africa and Asia

jackal

dingo—a wild dog that lives in Australia

dingo

coyote (kye-OH-tee)—an animal similar to a wolf; coyotes howl like wolves but have smaller bodies

coyote

Meet the Breeds

Dogs live everywhere on Earth. The American Kennel Club® keeps track of purebred dogs in the United States. They place the breeds into seven different groups.

SPORTING
Sporting dogs are very active and make good hunting dogs.

Labrador retriever

(LAB-ruh-dor ri-TREE-vur) a large dog with black, yellow, or brown fur; Labrador retrievers are popular pets and hunting dogs

pointer

a medium-sized dog with a short coat; pointers help hunters find birds by holding still and facing in the direction of the bird

golden retriever

a medium-sized dog with shaggy, gold-colored hair; golden retrievers want to please their owners

TOY Toy dogs are bred mainly as pet lap dogs.

Chihuahua

(chi-WAH-wuh)—the world's smallest dog; it stands 5 inches (13 centimeters) tall at the shoulders and has short or long hair

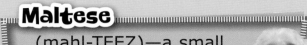

Maltese

(mahl-TEEZ)—a small dog with long white, silky hair; the Maltese was probably the world's first lap dog

Yorkshire terrier

(YORK-shur TER-ee-ur)—a small dog with long hair; Yorkies were first used to kill rats in England in the mid-1800s

pug

a dog with short hair, a flat, wrinkled face, and a curled tail; pugs came from China

HOUND Hounds are often used as hunting dogs. They hunt by sight and smell.

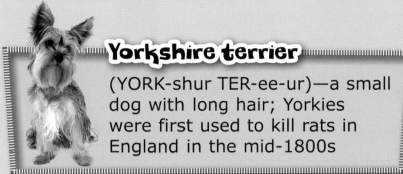

dachshund

(DOX-uhnt)—a small dog with a long body and short legs; the hot dog was named after the dachshund because of its shape

beagle (BEE-guhl)

a small dog with short legs, long ears, and a smooth coat; beagles are often kept as pets or used to hunt rabbits

greyhound

a dog with a thin body and smooth fur; the greyhound is the fastest dog breed and can run up to 45 miles (72 kilometers) per hour

HERDING

Herding dogs can round up animals such as cattle and keep them together. They sometimes even herd people!

German shepherd

a large dog with pointed ears, a narrow nose, and black, brown, or gray fur; German shepherds make good guard and police dogs

Old English sheepdog

a breed of large dog with long hair that hangs over its eyes; its fur is gray, blue, or white

collie

(KAH-lee)—a dog with thick fur that can be long or short; collies have long noses and narrow heads

TERRIER

Dogs in the Terrier group have lots of energy. Their ancestors hunted rats, mice, and other small animals.

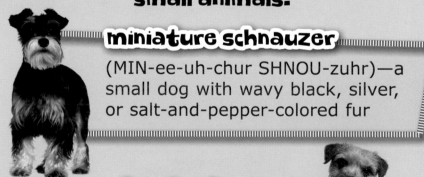

miniature schnauzer

(MIN-ee-uh-chur SHNOU-zuhr)—a small dog with wavy black, silver, or salt-and-pepper-colored fur

border terrier

a medium-sized dog with wiry fur; the border terrier was bred to hunt foxes

bull terrier

a medium-sized dog with short fur and an egg-shaped head

WORKING
Working dogs are very helpful to people. Some guard buildings or find missing people.

boxer

a dog with short fur, strong legs, and big eyes; boxers stand on their hind legs and "box" with their front legs

Great Dane

a large dog that has long legs and a short coat; the Great Dane was first used to hunt wild boar

rottweiler

(RAHT-wye-lur)—a strong black and brown dog with short hair, often used as a guard dog

NON-SPORTING

Breeds that don't fit into the other groups are placed in the non-sporting group.

poodle

a smart dog with thick, curly hair; poodles range in size from the fairly large standard poodle to the tiny toy poodle

bulldog

a strong dog with a round head, powerful jaws, and short legs; the bulldog was first used to fight bulls in Great Britain

dalmatian

(dal-MAY-shuhn)—a dog breed that has a white coat and black or brown spots; dalmatians are born white and get their spots about four weeks after birth

Designer Dogs and Mutts

What do you get when you mate two different purebred dogs? A designer dog! Designer dog breeders hope their offspring will have the best traits of each breed.

breeder

a person who raises dogs to sell; good breeders make sure to choose healthy parent dogs to have puppies; breeders should also have vets check the puppies for health problems that designer dogs sometimes have

Labradoodle

a Labrador retriever mixed with a poodle; Labradoodles have straight, wavy, or curly hair

Yorkipoo

a Yorkshire terrier mixed with a toy poodle; these smart dogs are best with adults and older children

goldendoodle

a golden retriever mixed with a poodle; goldendoodles enjoy playing outside

puggle

a pug mixed with a beagle; puggles have a good sense of smell

cockapoo

a cocker spaniel mixed with a poodle; cockapoos are friendly and get along well with other pets

mutt

a dog that comes from several unknown breeds; more than half of all pet dogs in the United States are mutts

Chorkie

a Chihuahua mixed with a Yorkshire terrier; because of their small size, Chorkies do well in apartments

Chiweenie

a Chihuahua mixed with a dachshund; the Chiweenie's nickname is the "Mexican taco"

Morkie

a Maltese mixed with a Yorkshire terrier; Morkies have lots of energy

From Puppy to Dog

Dogs begin life as helpless puppies. They need their mothers to feed them and keep them safe as they grow.

life cycle

the series of changes that takes place in a living thing, from birth to death; dogs give birth to live young

nest

the female dog chooses a place to give birth, such as a soft blanket

membrane

(MEM-brane)—a thin, flexible layer of skin that covers a newborn puppy; the female licks her puppies to remove the membrane and help them breathe

life span

the number of years a dog usually lives, depending on its breed; smaller breeds usually live longer than larger breeds

whelp (WELP)—to give birth; the female gives birth after carrying her puppies for two months

puppy puppies can't see or hear for the first few weeks of life

litter a group of puppies born at the same time to the same mother; female dogs can give birth to two litters each year

A Dog's Body

Some dogs have curly tails and fluffy fur. Others have long noses and pointy ears. No matter what they look like, all dogs share similar body parts.

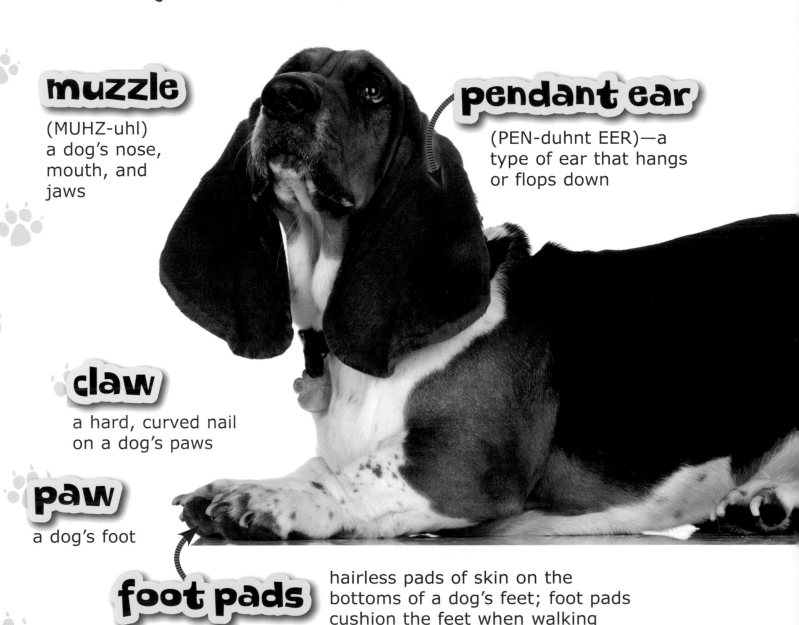

muzzle

(MUHZ-uhl) a dog's nose, mouth, and jaws

pendant ear

(PEN-duhnt EER)—a type of ear that hangs or flops down

claw

a hard, curved nail on a dog's paws

paw

a dog's foot

foot pads

hairless pads of skin on the bottoms of a dog's feet; foot pads cushion the feet when walking

pricked ear
a type of ear that stands straight up; pricked ears collect sounds better than floppy ears

canine
(KAY-nyn)—a long, pointed tooth; dogs tear food with their canine teeth

withers
(WITH-urs)—the tops of an animal's shoulders; a dog's height is measured from the ground to the withers

coat
a dog's fur; most dogs shed their fur in fall and spring

tail
dogs use their tails to keep steady and not fall over; they also communicate with their tails

Keeping Your Dog Healthy

Dogs are loving, loyal, and fun. They depend on their owners to keep them safe. With regular checkups and grooming, dogs can live healthy lives.

groom

to clean and make a dog look neat; dogs should be bathed monthly and brushed weekly; dogs that shed a lot may need to be brushed every day

pin brush

a brush with long metal pins that remove dead hair; used to brush long-haired dogs

greyhound comb

a brush with wide teeth on one end and narrow teeth on the other end; used to remove tangles from a dog's fur

dog shampoo

dogs should be washed with shampoo made for dogs; human shampoo dries out a dog's skin

nail clipper

used to trim a dog's nails; nails are too long if they touch the floor while the dog is standing

clean ears

your dog's ears should be clean and pink on the inside; gently clean them monthly with ear cleaner and a cotton ball

shedding rake

a rakelike comb used to brush shedding dogs

hound glove

used for brushing dogs with smooth coats, such as boxers or greyhounds

veterinarian

(vet-ur-uh-NER-ee-uhn)
a doctor who treats sick or injured dogs; veterinarians also help dogs stay healthy

checkup

a visit to the vet to make sure your pet is healthy; dogs should see the veterinarian every year for a checkup

canine toothpaste

toothpaste for dogs comes in flavors like chicken and beef; it's also safe for dogs to swallow

finger brush

a toothbrush with bristles that fits over your finger like a glove; dog owners should brush their dogs' teeth every day

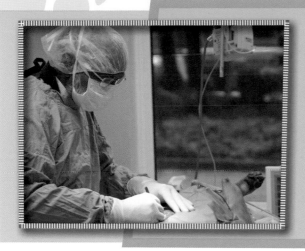

spay

to operate on a female dog so it is unable to produce young

neuter

(NOO-tur)—to operate on a male dog so it is unable to produce young

vaccination

(vak-suh-NAY-shun)—a shot of medicine that protects dogs from a disease

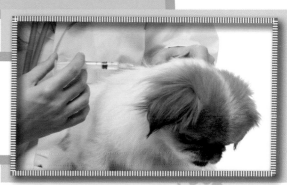

kennel

(KEN-uhl) a cage made of plastic or wire; dogs sleep and rest in kennels

dog house

a small, outdoor house that keeps dogs safe from the cold and rain

Dog Behavior

Why do dogs bark? Pant? Chase their tails? These common doggie behaviors might seem strange to us. But they're what make dogs dogs!

train

to teach a dog how to behave; owners teach their dogs to go to the bathroom outside; dogs also learn how to sit, stay, and come

lick

dogs lick their owners to show affection

instinct

(IN-stingkt)—behavior that is natural rather than learned; much of a dog's behavior is guided by instinct

pack animal

dogs are pack animals; they need to be with people or other dogs

bite

dogs bite to keep their owners safe or if they feel afraid; never walk up to a dog you don't know

chase tail

puppies chase their tails for fun

wag tail

dogs shake their tails back and forth when they're happy or alert; dogs tuck their tails between their legs when they are afraid or nervous

pant

to breathe quickly with an open mouth; dogs pant to cool off because they don't sweat

mark

dogs claim their territory by marking it with their urine; these marks let other dogs know who's been there

bark

dogs bark when they are happy, angry, hurt, or afraid; they even bark to say hello!

Dog Senses

Dogs explore their world by sniffing everything they see. They perk up their ears at the quietest of sounds. Dogs are always on the lookout.

wet nose

a dog's wet nose traps smells; dogs are able to smell odors that people can't, such as gases or drugs

whisker

(WISS-kur)—a long stiff hair growing on a dog's muzzle, cheeks, and over the eyebrows; whiskers help dogs feel for small objects they can't easily see

Jacobson's organ

(JAY-kuhb-suhnz OR-guhn)—an organ above the roof of a dog's mouth used to smell **pheromones**; dogs may be able to "smell" emotions using this organ

pheromone

(FER-uh-mohn)—a smell produced by an animal; animals use these smells to communicate

frequency

(FREE-kwuhn-see)—the number of sound waves that pass a location in a certain amount of time; dogs hear sounds at frequencies that people can't

sound wave

a wave or vibration that can be heard

night vision

dogs see better at night than people do because their eyes let in more light

detect

(di-TEKT)—to notice or find something; some dogs can use their noses to detect cancer in human urine and breath

scent receptor

(SENT ri-SEP-tuhr)—a cell in the nose that gathers smells; dogs have 220 million scent receptors; people have 5 million

color-blind

unable to tell certain colors apart; red and green look the same to dogs; they can see blue, yellow, and gray

Playful Pooches

Dogs just want to have fun! Exercise your dog to keep it happy and healthy.

collar

(KAH-lur)—a thin band of leather or other material worn around a dog's neck

leash

(LEESH)—a strap used to hold and control dogs; dogs should be kept on leashes when out for a walk

identification tag
(eye-den-tuh-fuh-KAY-shuhn TAYG)—a tag that lists a dog's name and its owner's phone number; the tag is attached to the collar

chew toy
puppies who are teething need safe chew toys; chewing soothes sore mouths

microchip
(MYE-kroh-chip)—a tiny device placed between a dog's shoulder blades, under the skin; the chip holds the dog's ID and can be scanned by vets or animal shelters

fetch

a game in which an owner throws a ball or a stick, and the dog brings it back

dog life vest

a life vest that keeps dogs safe while swimming

exercise

(EK-suhr-syz)—a physical activity done in order to stay healthy and fit; all dogs need exercise

dog park

a park where dogs can play off the leash and meet other dogs

tug-of-war

a game in which a dog and its owner pull on either side of a rope; a rope with knots on both ends works best

Dog Shows and Contests

Running through tunnels! Jumping into the water! Dog shows and contests give our four-legged friends the chance to show off their skills.

obedience

(oh-BEE-dee-uhnss)—dogs must obey rules and commands given by their owners

tracking

dogs must find objects placed in an open field by following their scents

agility

(uh-GIL-uh-tee) dogs must move quickly and easily over jumps, through tunnels, and around poles

conformation

(kon-for-MAY-shun)—a dog is given points based on how well it meets its breed standard; judges look at a dog's fur, teeth, and muscles

Canine Good Citizen ®

an award given by the American Kennel Club to dogs that follow commands and are friendly to strangers and other dogs

dock jumping

a contest where dogs jump off of a dock and into a pool; the dog that jumps the farthest wins!

hunting

dogs and hunters work together to find and kill prey; they are given points based on how well they perform

Feeding Fido

When food hits the bowl, dogs come running!
Dogs also need fresh, clean water at all times.

kibble

(KIB-buhl)—dry dog food; most dogs eat kibble

dog bowl

a bowl made out of clay, metal, or plastic used to hold a dog's food

food puzzle

a toy that holds dog food; a dog must figure out how to get the food out of the puzzle

wean

(WEEN)—to stop depending on a mother's milk; female dogs begin to wean their puppies when they are about three weeks old

carnivore

(KAHR-nuh-vohr)—an animal that eats only meat; dogs are mainly meat eaters

saliva

(suh-LYE-vuh) the clear liquid in a dog's mouth; dogs don't often chew their food; the food is coated with saliva and swallowed whole

poisonous

(POI-zuhn-uhss)—able to kill or harm if swallowed; chocolate, raisins, grapes, nuts, onions, and sugarless gum are poisonous to dogs

vitamin

(VYE-tuh-min)—a nutrient that helps keep dogs healthy; puppies should not be given vitamins; they get vitamins from their puppy food

obesity

(oh-BEE-si-tee)—to be extremely overweight; overweight dogs live shorter lives; dogs shouldn't be overfed or given table scraps

Dogs on the Job

Did you know that some dogs have jobs?
They work with police and visit sick people.
Some dogs are even Hollywood stars!

guide dog

a dog that helps guide people who can't see or who have trouble seeing

therapy dog

(THER-uh-pee DAWG) a dog that visits people who are sick or hurt; therapy dogs help people who are in need

search and rescue dog

a dog trained to help find people who are lost, missing, or trapped

herding dog

a dog that controls the movements of other animals by leaping, barking, and nipping at their heels; herding dogs often herd farm animals such as sheep

police dog

a dog trained to help police officers; German shepherds, rottweilers, and Labrador retrievers all work as police dogs

hunting dog

a dog that helps hunters find game; retrievers pick up dead animals and bring them back to the hunter; spaniels chase birds out of bushes

television and movie dog

a dog trained to act in movies, TV shows, and commercials

sled dog

a dog trained to pull sleds through snow and ice; some sled dogs also compete in races

Read More

Hutmacher, Kimberly M. *I Want a Dog.* I Want a Pet. Mankato, Minn.: Capstone Press, 2012.

Jordan, Apple. *Guess Who Sniffs.* Guess Who. New York: Marshall Cavendish Benchmark, 2012.

Slade, Suzanne. *Why Do Dogs Drool? And Other Questions Kids Have about Dogs.* Kids' Questions. Minneapolis: Picture Window Books, 2010.

Internet Sites

FactHound offers a safe, fun way to find Internet sites related to this book. All of the sites on FactHound have been researched by our staff.

Here's all you do:

Visit *www.facthound.com*

Type in this code: 9781429685726

Super-cool stuff! Check out projects, games and lots more at **www.capstonekids.com**